CW00666124

EDVARD HAGERUP GRIEG

LYRIC PIECES & POETIC TONE-PICTURES

Op.12 & Op.3

Edited by Angus Morrison

THE ASSOCIATED BOARD OF THE ROYAL SCHOOLS OF MUSIC

INTRODUCTION

As I said in my foreword to the two volumes of pieces by Grieg, which I selected and edited for the Associated Board some years ago, the task of editing his music is in many ways an easy one. He was a wonderful craftsman, and all through his life, from the earliest published works onwards, his exactness of notation was beyond reproach. If one takes the trouble to play exactly what he wrote – meticulously observing every note value, every rest, every mark of expression – one has gone a long way towards acquiring the right approach to playing his music.

I have added a certain amount of fingering but practically nothing in the way of phrasing or expression. Those few markings not in the original editions are always printed in brackets.

Pedalling is a more difficult matter. There is no question that Grieg demanded a greater awareness of the pedal, and a more advanced use of it, than is normally found in the beginner of the present day; but provided the pupil can actually *reach* the pedal and has a sensitive ear, there seems no reason to prevent his using it to excellent effect. I have added some supplementary indications (again always in brackets) but the student must develop initiative in this respect, as the overall effect of these pieces can be considerably enhanced if the sustaining pedal is used with skill and discrimination.

With regard to ornaments, there are very few in either of these two sets of pieces. The grace-notes in Op.12, Nos.3 & 4 and in Op.3, No.5 should, I suggest, be played *before* the beat, while it seems more in keeping with the mood of Op.12, No.7 for them to be played very lightly *on* the beat. In Op.12, No.5 the turns can equally be played on or before the beat according to the taste of the player – one should not be too dogmatic in these matters, especially in romantic music – although there is evidence that Grieg himself favoured a basically classical on-the-beat treatment of turns and ornaments.

The first volume of *Lyric Pieces*, Op.12 was published in 1867 when the composer was 24, and are – with the exception of some of the folk-song arrangements from Op.17 – the easiest pieces Grieg ever wrote. I think there can be little doubt that they were a conscious attempt to provide attractive material for the beginner, somewhat on the lines of Schumann's *Album for the Young*.

The *Poetic Tone-Pictures*, Op.3 were published two years earlier, in 1864 when the composer was only 21. They are generally more difficult than Op.12, but even so there is nothing in them that should be beyond the range of Grade 6/7 standard. It has been said that these earlier pieces are more conventional in style and do not show the markedly nationalistic features of his later music. It seems to me, however, that many of his 'musical fingerprints' are already strongly in evidence – particularly the very characteristic cadences in No.2 and the falling leading-notes in No.5 – musical traits that were to feature in almost everything he wrote, and which make his highly individual style so attractive and so immediately recognisable to the sensitive musician.

ANGUS MORRISON
London, 1983

Dedicated to Fräulein Betty Egeberg

LYRIC PIECES
Arietta

Poco Andante e sostenuto

GRIEG, Op. 12

Waltz

Allegro moderato

Watchman's Song

(composed after a performance of Shakespeare's 'Macbeth')

Molto Andante e semplice

Dance of the Elves

Molto Allegro e sempre staccato

AB 1814

Folk-song

Con moto [sempre cantabile e legato]

5

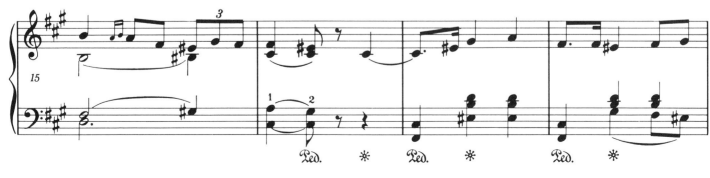

morendo

mf

morendo

[♩ = c. 88]

Norwegian Air

Album-leaf

Song of the Fatherland

Dedicated to Herr Benjamin Feddersen

POETIC TONE-PICTURES

GRIEG, Op. 3

Allegro, ma non troppo

Allegro cantabile

2

[sempre col. Ped.]

poco string.

dimin.

poco rit.

a tempo

poco string.

dim.

poco rit.

più vivo

[senza Ped.]

[♩ = c. 54]

24

Con moto

AB 1814

Andante con sentimento

4

Allegro moderato

5

Vivo

AB1814

BLANK PAGE